Copies may be ordered direct:

Send **$ 19.95** prepaid (includes mailing/handling) to:

Proteus / LA
12201 Stewarton Drive
Porter Ranch, CA 91326

Or call Toll-Free: **(800) 484-9971 xt 6633**

Visit our Website : www.proteusla.com

LOS ANGELES : CITY OF DREAMS

Up The Mellow Yellow Brick Road

Mark St. George

Proteus

LOOKING BACK TO THE FUTURE

In a letter to a New York publisher sometime in 1972, I presented a book
(then called THE CITY) as ". . .a literary work that effectively synthesizes the
polarizing elements currently making the cultural scene-- encompassing at
once MacLuhan and Mailer, Jesus and Marx, Angela and Agnew, Apollo and
Dionysus, Manson and Nixon, Binary Gods and Welfare Rolls, Ms. American
Pie and Martha Mitchell."   Also: "It is what you would call 'hot copy'-- a
psychedelic celebration of life, where poetry and politics converge in a cosmic
whole greater than the sum of its parts."

Yes, well.

The idea that LA is or can be taken to be the Big Picture was not a new one,
even in 1972. But perhaps nowhere else on the planet could you find the "full
menu" of urban lifestyles. Looking back, from the edge of the New Millenium,
the 60s and 70s come to life as a time when all seemed gloriously
changeable and even permissible-- before Reagan and Star Wars, before
AIDS and Political Correctness, before Nintendo and MTV and the Web.

This book is published to re-capture and celebrate those charismatic years.
And to come to a realization that what is truly good and honorable about
ourselves lies buried in golden moments ripe for recollection. By looking
back, we pass through a door (or window) into pathways, both real and
virtual, leading into the Garden.

But that's another story.

Mark St. George

CONTENTS

ACTION

FREEWAY
RR
LAX
SURFERS
TRIBAL DANCE
COLISEUM
FAST BREAK
BODY ENGLISH
HEAVYWEIGHTS
CENTER COURT
HOLLYWOOD PARK
JOGGERS
SINGLES MIX
BIKERS
TRAVELLERS

RITUAL

DELIVERY
THE CONSUMERS
THE WORSHIPPERS
HOUSEWIVES AND HOOKERS
SENIOR CITIZENS
SUPERSTARS
COUNTY BARS
TRIPPING
SWINGING
COURTROOM
DUTY
BRIGHT ANGELS
UNEMPLOYMENT LINE
5TH STREET
TOGETHER
MOURNING
GENERATION
GETTING OFF
CIRCUITRY

VISION

GATHERING OF THE TRIBES
VISION IN MOTION
ANGEL DUST
COSMIC BIRTH

Acknowledgment

The Author wishes to thank the various sources for providing additional
images for inclusion in this book. Particular credits are noted as follows:

The text and photographs in this book relate to a time period
in Los Angeles spanning the late 60sand 70s.

Cover Design by : VanHook Studios

This book is for :

angels of the city

THE CITY

through
the looking glass
slowly
euphoric seekers
warp their way
toward

the city

beyond
the blur of crusted ritual
and
neon moonscapes
shimmering
beneath the midday sun
and
the faustian cadence of
the marketplace
spinning
through
tax-sheltered modes
along
dialectic roads
of
evolution

beyond
patterned forms of
scarcity
and
primal trust deeds

divinely stored
in
stainless vaults
and
the siren-wail of freeway demons
casting
parabolic shadows
onto
sleek dichondra lawns
while
neocorporate yawns
flash
their binary message code
in
absolution

the mirror shift
where
vision
feeds upon itself
in
cosmic deja-vu
and
the brightest and the best
scan
the universal residue
for
psychic fragments
streaking
in suspension

along
inverse dimensions
of
form and function
at
the junction
of
a yellow brick road
beaming
charismatic angel dust
for
tribal brothers and sisters
orbiting a primal core
of
generation
to turn
the existential trick
called

: : :THE CITY: : :

it
isn't very
hard to find
if
you don't mind
travelling
for
as long as it
takes

PLACES

DOWNTOWN

the
clear-eyed seekers
who
came here first
having crossed the desert
dry with thirst
were right-on hardy
pioneers
gone awol from
their
eastern peers

they
set up house
in the LA basin
ma and pa and cousin jason
tilled the soil
and
chased the sun

and that was how
the west was won

then each generation
played its hand
with
its table stakes of
bread and land
dealing
perpetuity

with
frontier hospitality

then
the railroad came
and industry
and the dealers charged a higher fee
as migrant gamblers
took their chance
with sweaty palms and baggy pants

the coming of the new technology
demanded skills
that
sent the big dealers off to the hills
to clip coupons and dividend checks
and grudgingly reshuffle
the decks

the downown casinos they
left behind
became a mecca for
the visionary blind
as
the common folk were left to dwell
in the vacuum of
a corporate shell

the downtown scene is changing fast
a variation of its
recent past
emerging as a medium-cool melting pot
for those who have
and those who
have not

HOLLYWOOD BOULEVARD

you
won't always find
a straight line
from the ozarks
to bel air
nor the shortest distance
between sioux falls
and beverly hills
for instance

(some say it's shorter if not straighter
from the bronx)

on route 66
you can reach the coast
in a vw camper or a greyhound bus
but sooner or later
you'll be dining at george's
with hometown news
from the stand
on las palmas

the ashtrays runneth over
at the gold cup
the ranch market
never closes
mark twain is a hotel
if you can't afford
the lido
or the montecito

the chinese is for tourists
the real show is on the boulevard
24 hours
lean hungry lads
in see-through knits
maidens with corn-fed tits
peddling strange flowers

the cowboys
on the boulevard
ride hard
from sun up to sundown
and way past

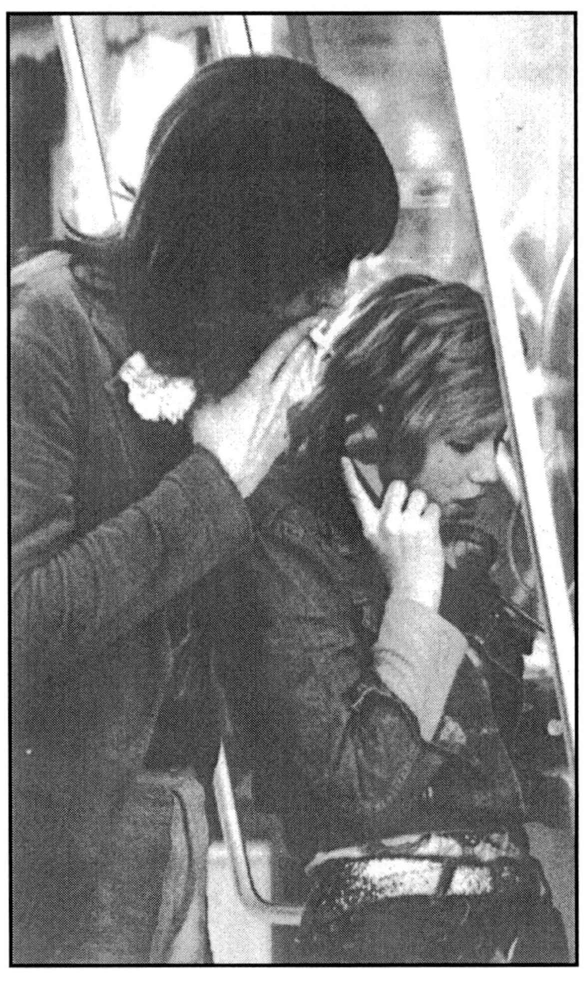

guitars
and okie bars
between each roundup
make
young guns fast

(much too fast for mgm)

be kind
to your waitress
she once
had a vision
world war ii debutantes
you will find
high-strutting
on the boulevard
in
max factor and hot pants

(tomorrow the candy store)

high above

the smog and traffic

grooving

territorial imperatives and vintage wines

among

fair-weather canyons and velvety lawns

god's own euphoric children

seek

their cosmic apogee

with

each hip trajectory

of

the dow jones

corporate heads and fashion-chic radicals

clipping celestial coupons

in

pucci gowns and studded levis

chase

the california sun

with

fun and games

while the names

at

dinner parties

sport

charismatic

roman numerals

linear generations

of

the brightest and the best

survive the test
of
protesting ethic and dissenting drummers
mirror-shifting
in
hip configurations
of
yellow submarines and chauffeured limousines
toward a
universal pantomime of perpetuity
and
happy days
along
sequestered walkways
in
the land of oz

THE COAST

the
end of the road
travelled by
many a seeker from the east
stretches
along its sandy crescent
like
some restive primal beast
white-hot
in the sun
cradling a playful surf
with its
belly

sleek
erotic gulls
trace
fleeting noon shadows
soaring
high above the sand
from
point dume to palos verdes
and
on a clear day you can see
catalina
from
the palisades among
colonnades

of palms and high-rise
condominiums

shimmering
along hermosa and
santa monica
shores

pale
enchanted dreamers
shake their journeymen's dust
from
weary feet
and run
to take their place
in the sun
beside
bronze brothers and sisters

CITY HALL

in
the eleventh hour
the manic race for
affluence
pursued by age-old precedents
seeks its twilight apogee
and
spinning through
like some demented fiery wheel
consumes again
pandora's seal

great howling winds of scarcity
amplified
through the eye of instant time
sees the climb
of

demonic shadows of unreason
while
a distant vision seeks precision

mellowing through a binary gateway
of common law and
contributory affluence and
the rights of free rotarians
stepping past the hollow blast
of
faustian drummers

it might be
the eleventh hour
will last
forever

WARNERS' THEATRE

THE STUDIO

when
the dream-weavers came out west
many years ago
little did they know
that in their quest for money and fame
there dripped some love and sorrow
in their breast
and that
the monuments they built
overpaid in labor and guilt
would survive
their founders' name

for lo and behold
a child as born
here amid the cactus and corn

growing
in stature until he stood
tall enough to be called
hollywood

then
the common folk throughout the land
held their breath as the camera panned
and
young and old forgot their prayers
to god
and followed their players
reliving
classic tales
of yesteryear

and
as every reel unwound
shopgirls and cabbies shorted their rent
for

an afternoon of entertainment
in celebration of
the fusion of
sight and sound

PRESENTING :

heroic deeds and social needs
reality and fantasy
moral themes and moonbeams
sentiment and merriment
blood and lust
and boredom too
from
HOLLYWOOD
to me and you

but there came a time
in postwar years
bringing truth to
growing fears
of a rival
born
of tecnology
a classy lass of circuitry

pampered
by admen for
mouthwash and brewers
she became the sweetheart of
millions of viewers

the aging dream-weavers
were
out of sorts

as they crumpled up
their financial reports
of
dwindling receipts and empty seats
all brought
to the edge of doom
by
the electronic lady
in our living room

and so there came to be a
marriage of necessity as the
painful thorn in the studios' side was
blessed as hollywood's electronic bride

now they each will do their thing in a
funky intermedia happening
writing yet another page
in a consumer-oriented age

it is rumored they have a step-child
bred to be
the Supermedium of All Time
as new-world natives pay their dues and
gather phosphorescent cues
to stand macluhan's dictum

on its head
substituting content
for form instead

SUNSET STRIP

if
you're a night people and
you don't make
eighty grand a year
you'll tire of new york someday
and somehow find your way
out west
where adventure comes
casually dresed
in
leather and suede and
clairol blondes who
masquerade
the rural twang of
barnyard blues
with rock and cock and angel dust
and don't you know
amyl nitrite is a must
to really get your head
together
and it don't matter none
whether or not

the brand of pot
you smoke
is homegrown
it's worth a toke or two
to
bring out the wild man
in you

the flower children
on the strip
have come and gone
not with a whimper but with
a yawn
they've gone home to
communes-in-the-sky
with
mellowing drummers
and perpetual high

the dress extras that remain
can't be sure if they're
spaced-out
or sane

THE VALLEY

just over the hill from

the LA basin

transplanted middle americans

sporting

double-knit sunshaded native fashions

tend

autistic entrepreneurial trees

to sieze
tomorrow's giant green jolly scene
within
the suburban bedroom sprawl
of
the valley

hyperkinetic hemi-charged superkids
roar down
sunflower-powered cannabistic freeway lanes
hi-riding with the sun in
quadrasonic overkill
to fill
psychic chords with primal boards
lo-riding between tokes
from
canoga park and sherman oaks to
the malibu surf

junior misses
learn to roll
while rocking as they
stroll
from
neat dichondra lawns
through
rainbow-colored dawns
beneath
the watchful eye of
mom
grooming poppies for
the prom
in celebration of new harvests with
the
weatherman

L A COUNTRY CLUB

god bless the child

who has his

own

snugly breast-feeding

bullish portfolios

wrapped in swaddling double-knit

plus-fours

rocking to the stereophonic beat of

rococo drummers

scoring

binary light shows

within

a neocorporate manger

god bless the child

who shares his

toys

with puppy dogs and colored boys

dealing

a slice of the GNP

among

a stoned majority

while

new-world natives

weaned

on playboy centerfolds

pound

at the gates of the polo lounge

and brown-shoed media scanners

detect
distant blimps
godalmighty fellows
an army of lumpenschleppers
slouching toward
sun city

and
somewhere near the 14th green
ghostly cherubs make the scene
with
sleek irons and caddy carts
while
the unborn catcher-in-the-rye
is but a twinkling in
the computer's eye

LA BREA TAR PITS

some lazy summer afternoon
when you tire of
disneyland and magic mountain
and the creatures at
the zoo
in some funny way laugh back
at you

when the crowd at steffanino's
won't admit
your conversation
and
the waiter at perino's
has misplaced your reservation
when
the world hangs heavy
on your mind
and the dow jones has been
unkind
come down to the tar pits
in summertime
in sunny summertime
and you will find

yourself peering through
a sleek wire fence
at the birthplace of LA's
first residents
far-out generations with flesh and blood
holding court
beneath the pleistocene mud

burping bubble-up vapors

all the while
just inside
the miracle mile

the wooly beasts resurrected there
you won't find
stuffed and mounted

the jonathan club

in your neighborhood pub
in fact you won't find them anywhere
and certainly not at

when you come to the tar pits
in summertime

in sunny summertime
you may reflect that
many generations hence
some weary traveller may pause before
a sleek wire fence
and peering through
see what remains
of
me and you
an oozing black residue
of life on this planet
and
the LA times
etched
in pale granite

MARINA

a little
salt water and sun
after
a week on the run
really gets it on for city dwellers

a little booze
and a catalina cruise
is a trip for
cpas and lady tellers

so why be bored
just jump aboard
your diesel twin or righteous sail
heaven can wait
for a low interest rate
happiness is unopened mail

the best friend you've got
is your
sleek new yacht
she never talks back at you

and if you
don't have the knack for
a starboard tack
just
open up
another can of brew

REAL & RICH

WATTS

when
the air hangs hot and sticky
undisturbed
by yet unborn santana winds
and
the lazy rap of auto horns
rises up and over
steaming rooftops and asphalt city streets
soft
beneath the careful tread
of catlike weekend shoppers
and
the playful shrieks of aging children
swirl about their rapid footsteps
within
stark courtyard walls
the older folk remember

when
the air roared hot and sticky
black retching billowing smoke clouds
spewing up from a fiery core of rage
overfanned by howling winds of scarcity

in a confrontation of the spirit

and
the spastic wail of firemen's horns
rising up and over burning rooftops
and asphalt city streets caressingly soft
beneath the hot blood of native sons

in a celebration of the spirit

and
the playful shrieks of primal children
swirling through armed barricades
their rapid footsteps lit by firelight
in search of souvenirs among the ashes

in a confirmation of the spirit

some say it was
a very good year

CENTURY CITY

shazam!
cried the prop mistress
on the back lot at 20th
and while
phthisic set designers
took a nap
between takes
fenestrated hostess cakes
rose skyward
bordered with alcoa wrap

now down
the avenue of the stars
corporate studs
ride
magic reams of negotiable paper
while
shopgirls-on-the-mall
mount a wall
of endless charge cards
marking time for happy hours
at
the century house
and on a clear day
futuristic city planners
scan
a far horizon
for visionary sites
already coruscating
with
triple-net
logarithmic projections

MASSAGE
SSAGE
ALL MAJOR
CREDIT
CARDS
AL
OIL CA
ACCEP
OPEN
24
HOURS
OPEN
24
HOURS

SAUNA · M
NES

MASSAGE PARLOUR

the joys of home and hearth
are not
the only ones
to soothe a man
family and friends and apple pie
are great you know
sunday drives and golf and poker games
before
the late late show
are happy hours for everyman

but
man the hunter and man the beast
will
have himself a
sportive feast
and after a day of herculean toil
against
faustian demons of the marketplace
anonymous hands will
soothe the brute
and
he will taste the forbidden fruit
of
sauna muzak booze and

a rub of mineral oil

he is too patrician for
the harlot's den and
too plebian for the polo lounge
so
he will close his eyes
and be caressed
and dream
the impossible dream
upon
a forgotten mother's
breast

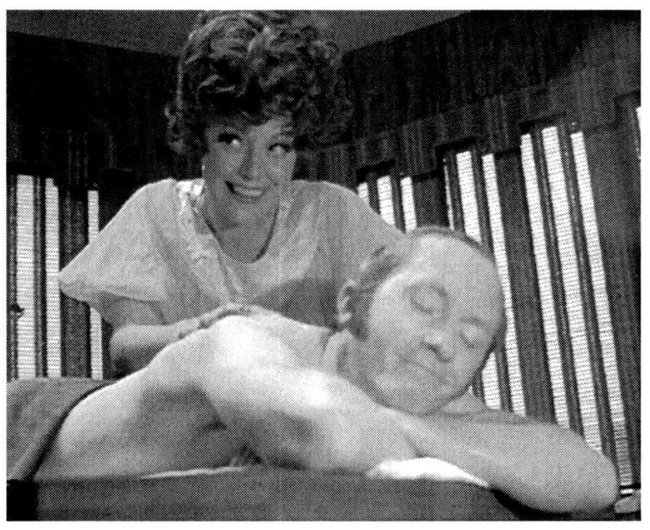

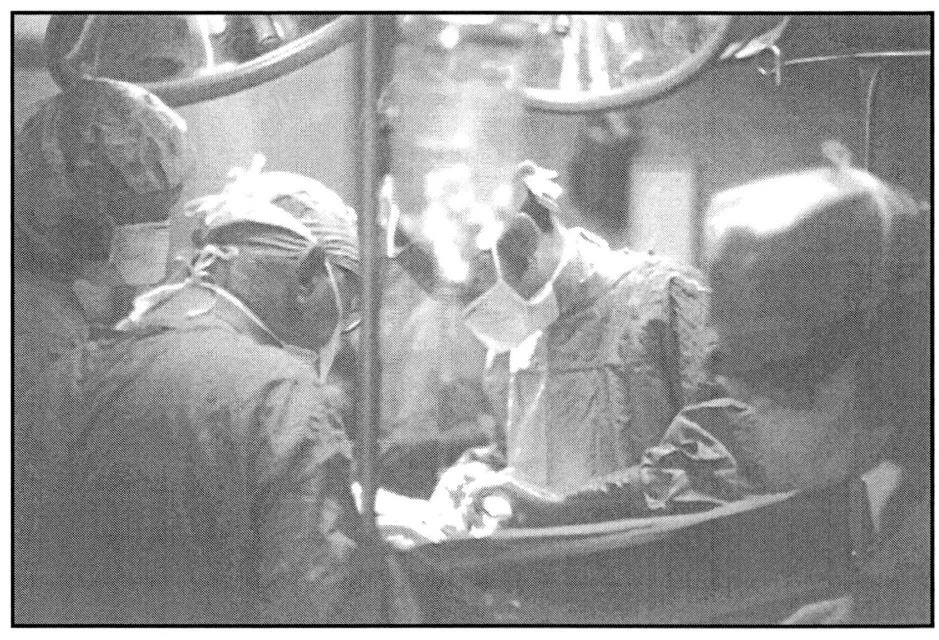

MEDICAL CENTER

time
beats a slow
cadence
within
these county walls
for
the residents
of
its antiseptic halls
while
a hovering angel
flaps
cybernetic wings
to ward off
evil happenings
passing
in the night
within sight
of
freeway demons

merciful healers
tend
their broken flock
around
the clock
tolling
an occasional bell
within
the grand hotel
whenever

time runs out

while across town
specialists
make
the private scene
of practice
near
the golfing green
seeking
sleek tax-sheltered lanes
for
even higher
capital gains

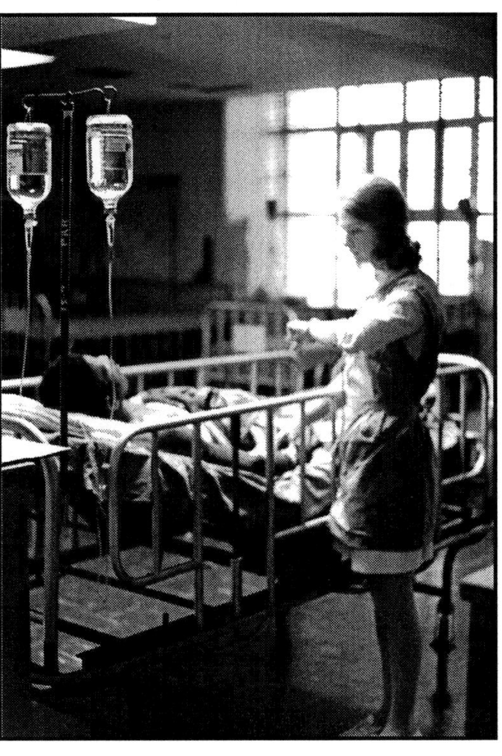

CAMPUS

streaking down
corridors
of
accelerating deja-vu
a point of you
mirror-shifts
its
binary message code
through
ivy hall and stadium walls

linear wisdom
fed by

hip monarchs in professorial robes
with a little help from
friendly foundations and
contributing angels
transmits
tomorrow's game plan
for
euphoric seekers in
poly-sci and sigma chi

as
dissenting drummers
pound
a different tune
for brothers and sisters
newly weaned on
protesting ethics and quadrasonic rock
and
superstars

right on
through
mellow semesters
of
keats and freud and macluhan and mailer
gaining somewhat
in translation
fed by
halftime scores and midnight tokes and
supersex
tripping past
neon moonscapes
and
generational traps
of
wired information
balling
the milky way
down

sunflower-powered
cosmic freeways
to turn
the existential trick

WYVELL

you are
cordially invited
to attend
an
eternity
of
electromagnetic happenings
here
at forest lawn
and
everywhere
whenever
you
are ready

: : : rsvp : : :

FACES

CYRANO

MAYOR TOM

within
the eye of
instant time
linear generations
jog
through
rainbow-colored dawns
wired to
hip scenarios of
keynesian
perpetuity

while

tomorow's children
boys and girls of all reasons
weaned on
egalitarian vision and protest ethics
rock
to the cadence of
hyperkinetic drummers
chasing
solar wavelengths
along
a yellow brick road
past
fluted colonnades
and
neat dichondra lawns
toward
freeways
of
cosmic interchange

and so

mayor tom
will mount
the furies of the day
charging
through
binary gateways
and
cybernetic inner city canyons
to
seek out
the elusive

: : :AMERICAN DREAM: : :

SAM

sam
was known
to run a tidy ship
a
grass-roots captain
with a
big city grip
uptight liberals
and the eastern press
spouting
frontier rhetoric
in academic dress
didn't bother sam
none
he got
his work done
and led his flock
to chase
the sun

sam
knew
the texture of
change
when to replace
and
when to rearrange

he engineered
the pivotal scene
of civil dissent
with
neat government
to keep
los angeles green

and if
his foreign policy
and
common-sense philosophy
didn't rate
with heads
of state
it didn't bother sam
none
he got
his work done
and
led his flock
to chase
the
sun

MARILYN

marilyn
once made the scene
as our
reigning movie queen   social relevancy
a screen goddess   has
purring   raised its head
cinematic supervibes   to upstage
for   yesterday's rage
wistful lovers   of
within   perilous heroines
darkened ornate palaces

                                          but
screen kisses   now and then
and   after
lightly draped chiffon   dinner and wine
turned us on   when
in living color   the lights are dimmed
bringing
medium-hot excitement   :::MARILYN LIVES:::
to
the hometown boys   stirring
                                          once again
now   the honey of
the old hollywood   romance
has   as we
changed with the years   view her
in   on
dwindling fan mail and   the late show
plastic premieres
louella and hedda
are dead

JERRY

jerry

tells it like it is

far-out global happenings

with

instant wings

replay each day

in

wavelike mirrored form

passing through

a two-way view

of

events

speeding out of time

in their

evolutionary climb

to fill

an ever-expanding norm

peering through

the

two-way view

we

all become tribal players

turned on

in the

primal dawn of

intraglobal show biz

in communion with

the word

knowing that the word

became

an electronic scanner

that

dwelleth among us

MS COURTNEY

when
ms courtney strolls
along the shops of
rodeo drive
perennial groups
of
chauvinist studs
turn and
take
ready aim

through
their ever-inflamed
erectile
looking glass
they misjudge
alas
her sensual brow
and
nubile willowy form

for
ms courtney
walks
a righteous path
between
friedan's mystique and steinem's wrath

sharing
heady visions
of
executive suites and caucus seats
she knows
that love is more than
quick tricks
and that
the glory of
housewife-mother-maid
is not
necessarily
where it's at

ms courtney
doesn't smoke virginia slims
and if
you tell her
she's come a long way baby
you'll
very likely get
a karate chop
you know where

THE SEAL SENATE
STATE CALIFORNIA
ENATOR
L GREEN
RNIA LEGIS
ISTRICT
262

SENATOR GREENE

senator greene

is known

to make the scene

as

a champion of ordinary folk

justice tempered by civil liberties for

disenfranchised brothers and sisters

demands a fair slice

of the pie

within

an impatient computer's eye

while

conservative rhetoric is spoke

spawning

visions of edwardian bliss

the senate views

its triumphs on the late late show

while

a lean and hungry constituency

rocks the status quo

senator greene

knows that

time is on his side

and that

aging principles of common law

mellowing somewhat

in legislation

bring consolation

to

hip subscribers

of

king's dream

60

ALICE

alice
doesn't chase
white rabbits
she cops a look
in her listing book
to see
where elephants
roam
and she knows
which way the appraiser blows
long before the escrows close
and
which house is not
a home

dichondra cushions
form
her nesting place
as each
split-level-full-of-grace
is a pass
through
a broker's looking glass

ho-ho
said the pea to the pod
after
insurance salesmen
those in real estate
are closest
to god

DAVE

dave

is

a corporate man a decision maker

he rides

the cosmic crest

of our

electronic gateway west

a futuristic pioneer

within

a selectronic circuit breaker

sleek modes of relativity

shaped by

executive committee

orchestrate

apollo's strings

to widen

his celestial wings

as

clear-eyed engineers

seek

unexplored frontiers

beyond

a giant step

in outer space

where

apocalyptic visions

along a yellow brick road

beam

tomorrow's message code

BISTRO

BEAUTIFUL PEOPLE

the

boys and girls

who chase the sun

take their pleasures

on the run

weaving

deep-throated phantasies

through

opalescent rainbow dawns

pirouetting among

visions of rhinestone-studded grand hotels

and fender-driven last tangos

mirrored through

quadrasonic channels of euphoria

and chartered jets and tennis sets

and

superstars

ah but

all in all

you must admit

theirs is a life of grace and wit

and

in lieu of mannikins from royal beds

we have

our ultramobile thoroughbreds

who

although they lack

heraldic crests

fill the bill

as

america's guests

Fir
vest
Ba
KING

BIG JIM

big jim
is a vp
who holds the key
to
your daily bread
a
friendly banker
juggling timeless deposits
with
interest to compound
this hallowed ground
conveyed
in
god we trust

big jim is
a straight-shooter
his code don't follow no
yellow brick road
but
grooves ahead instead
tracing
the grand design
of
prime-rated visions on demand

money is debt
the textbooks say and you can bet
big jim
will take a close look at
those
who promise to
pay

ERITAGE WEST

MOSSIE

when
mossie
came out west
she
didn't mind the smog 'n' traffic
none

generations
of
baptist elders
rolling
down their gravel-throated ozark circuit
made
hollow sounds
among
the purple twilight hills

now
endless summers
make the scene
as
mossie keeps
the ashtrays clean
with a
personal touch
sharing
the golden mind-zap of
boss city
with her
select clientele
just like
one of the family

MARSHA

through the eye of
deja vu
a luminous host of superstars
beams
its faustian message code
in living color

born in this century
fashioned by
good old boys and hip autistic taste-makers
god's own client list
poppin-fresh doughboys ham-fisted brewers
steel-belted grabbers angelic pain healers
honest wheeler-dealers jacks in gourmet boxes ultra-lashed foxes
mind-zapping un-colas flyable lassies in rotary-powered chassies
transmits
its soft unhidden persuasion

a task for
MARSHA

*****MEDIA SUPERFOX*****
zapping
consumer demand
with
120,000,000 volts of supercool
shazam!
while
a deep-throated chorus of
sleek suburban housewives chants
its dies irae

I BUY
THEREFORE I AM

HARVEY

when
harvey meets his maker
in
that final roundup in the sky
rolls and rolls of celestial ticker tape
in instant reply
will recall
his fair-haired stay
down among
the bears and bulls
of
the dow jones corral

heavenly portfolios
of
far-out P-E ratios
will tally
harvey's volume trades
of
blue chips municipal bonds and pork bellies
for his share of
the eternal GNP
sanctioned
by the universal SEC

the cosmic merger
he will underwrite
will be a
new issue
cumulative preferred no par-value no refund
in
an open-ended
go-go fund

STANLEY

many a day in court
conducting
legalistic rituals
in defense of constitutional writ
to outwit
the blindfolded lady
have taught stanley
how judicial dies are cast
since he passed
the bar

probing
procedural gaps and crusted precedent
stanley
fights
demons of unreason
with
medium-cool awareness
to bring
affirmative judgment
for
new world natives

his big fear is that when
the blindfold is lifted
from
the lady's eyes
she
blinded by the sun
may drop her scales
and
run

PUSSYCAT
DEEP THROAT

FIRST NIGHTERS

in classic times
the king and queen
and
those who made the courtly scene
would
set aside affairs of state
and
designs of grievous weight
for
holidays of public sport

the urgency of subject claims
was postponed a bit
for
fun and games
sponsored by the royal court

then the music shifted

now
the strains are
quadrasonic
and
closet-camp has waxed
symphonic
and while
first-nighters groove in shells
of
electromagnetic decibels
the rest of us
share
circuses and bread
on our
electronic water bed

SISTER MARTINA

when
sister martina
set out to join the order
years ago
she wore her little girl's trousseau
a flower child
fresh with angelic hope and laundry soap
she took her vows
with neat unknitted brows and became a
bride of christ

pursuing
pure dominican virtues
along the stations of the cross
she trod safe paths between good and evil
with eucharistic vision scored by
beatific modes of gregorian chant

the passing years and silent salted tears
have drained somewhat the starch from her habit
as she
views with instant time the new-world pantomime
of tribal forms

even now some roman dilettante
begs the pope's ear
to fashion
a modish nouveau habit with
matching hot pants
for next year's line

gentle lady
let the horseman pass you by

RABBI ZELDIN

beneath
the california sun
this sweet promised land of milk and honey
rabbi zeldin
wields the sacred torah for his
hip congregation
transmitting the word
from
the primal covenant of yahweh and israel
to his
new world children

within
the temple walls
timeless rituals celebrate
generations of patient wanderings
beneath
the watchful eye of
the god of abraham and the god of moses and the god of isaiah
toward
the final sabbath beyond
survival

back east
they say the words of the prophets
are written on the subway walls
and tenement halls
but here
out west
the rabbis are blessed
with high holidays
where congregations runneth over with
the good and the faithful

DR. HARRIS

dr. harris
can tell pretty much where your head is at
because he's a shrink
you see
what you say and what you do
provide the clue
to
psychic discontent and inner-city anomie

since
dr. harris pledged
to serve the flight of brothers and sisters
toward the sun
he has seen
the classic viennese high noon
fade
into psychedelic afterglow
a twilight of
behavioral mechanics primal screamers and gestalt dynamics

but where
are the flames of yesteryear
gone baby gone

now
dr. harris reorients
to view the psychic shift
within
an electoronic cosmic drift
gathering
right-on mosaic fragments
to piece together a
brave new world

JUAN

down in the barrio
juan
and
his latino friends never made
the electric kool-aid
acid test

circled by flower children casting seeds
among
barren cornmeal and rosary beads
they marked impatient time beneath
the shadow of the great anglo god
scarcity

visions
of airbrushing america green
with
a fading psychedelic scene
somehow got lost in the translation
by
tear gas shells and shotgun pellets in
the smoky streets of east LA

juan
now moves past
the twilight haze of his macho days
to seek new paths among the anglo world
while
the electronic eye of the man
follows him everywhere
to keep
the gates of bel air
safe
in case the frito bandito strikes again

LAPD

through
the midnight hours
while
good burghers sleep
soundly
between protective sheets
an army of blue knights
LA's finest
softly cruises along
mean streets
riding
gaps of probability
down
cybernetic inner-city canyons
in pursuit of
felonious shadows

desperation
fed by
howling winds of scarcity
and
misdirected genes
perpetrate
autistic schemes
seeking
euphoric paths of retribution
against
law and order
and
good old boys
soft-shoeing endless cotillions
with
swan-throated foxy cover girls

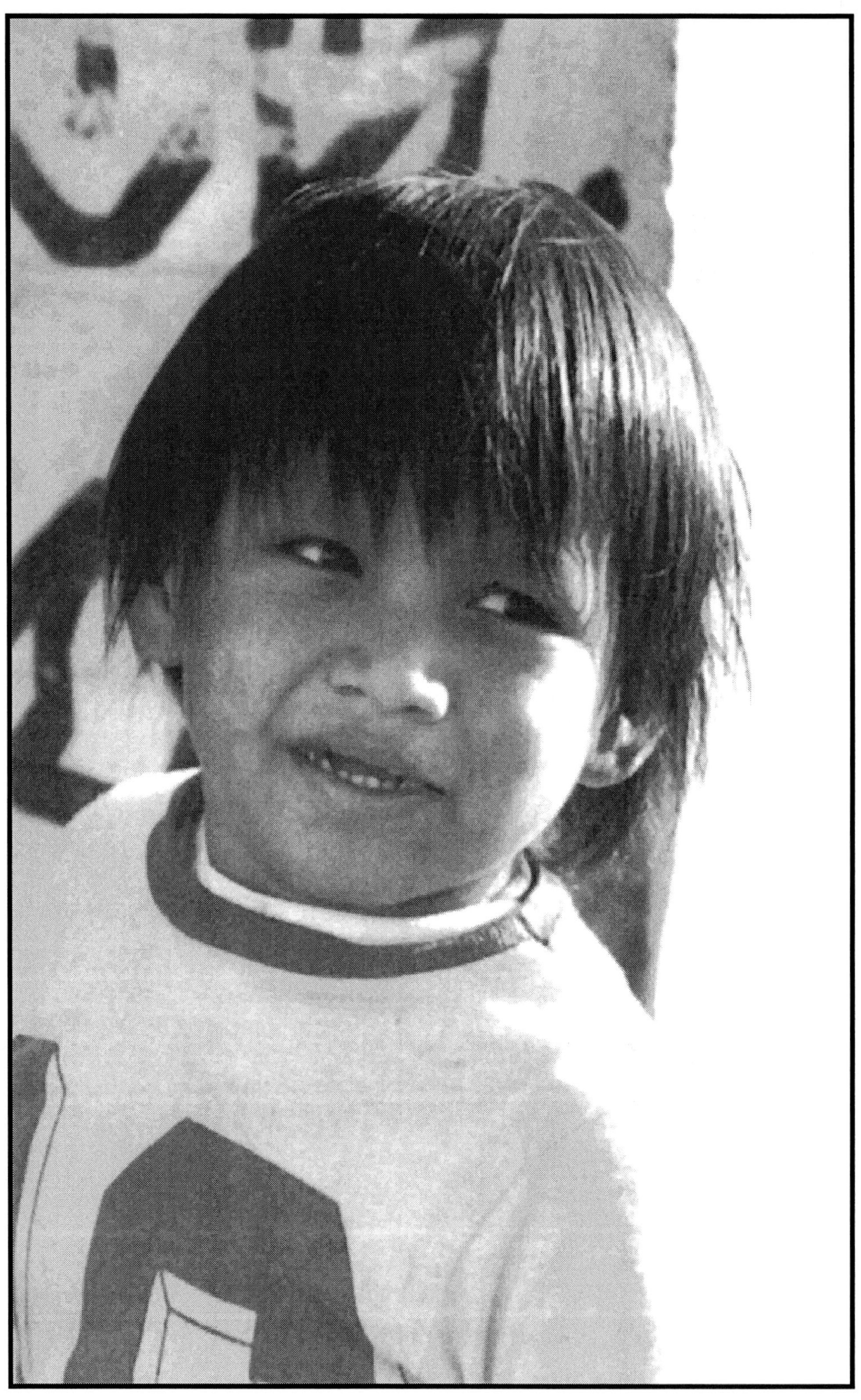

LITTLE FEATHER

children's games can be a drag for
little feather
older boys and girls have a way
of
type-casting as they play with toy guns
among
phantom mesquite plains and buffalo trails
in south central alleys

shielded by his tender years
little feather
plays his patterned red man's role
and
bites the dust in innocence
not knowing
his descent from proud tribal loins
ripped off by
firewater forked tongues government agents
greedy settlers uncle tomahwaks john wayne and kirk douglas

soon
little feather
will turn awkward pages
to learn the stages of his manhood
within
the white man's rituals

memories of childhood games
heated by tribal claims
beneath the california sun
may bring
little feather
much wisdom

JO-JO

jo-jo
is
a player
with
fashion-studded territorial imperatives
he shows
where
the action goes
anytime

jo-jo is
the man
hosting
visiting firemen and symposium speakers
errant cpas and executive streakers
with
a righteous stable of
superfine satin foxes
hi-steppin gals
in
boutique furs and gucci leather

jo-jo
makes the scene
in
his white-on-white limousine
dialing for dollars
with
an eye to
diff'rent strokes for
diff'rent folks

BAD BART

come friday
when the eagle flies
bad bart
stomps his way
past
steel columns and concrete-layered beams
out under the california sun
letting go his tennessee yell
full of
piss and vinegar

hellfire bo
another week of muscle and sweat gone by
time to spit in the boss' eye
and
get the wild man goin'

four hundred fifty seven cubic inches
roar through the LA basin
as bad bart
strokes his 4-on-the-floor
with
lats spread and deltoids rippling
and
hardhat flashing in the noonlight

nudie bars
and twanging guitars
bring visions of playboy centerfolds
through
the neon haze of
smoky joints and jack daniels
as bad bart

kicks a few asses
between glasses

he
aint never seen a woman he couldn't
burn down
and he don't care none for
whinin college pukes and pipe-smokin
phony-ass liberals and if
them limp-wristed
glitter freaks try 'n take over
why then
that's when
the shit's really goin to hit the fan

SED CA

CHIPS

                    did you ever
                  buy a set of wheels
                       from
                     this man

                  in-line six or V-8
                       chips
                  will put you together

              don't be afraid to make a deal
              buy sell or trade any automobile

              he'll pay top dollar for your edsel
          sell you a cherry lincoln way back of book
                not everybody can pay cash
                        so
                          a small down payment's
                             all you need

                  why tool around
                in your worn-out clunker
                cars like clohes make the man
              get your kicks and turn on the chicks
                       with
              a traffic-beatin' freeway eatin'
              4-on-the-floor quad-throated roar
              overhead cam and oversize bore
                easy-ridin' supermachine
              lowest payments you've ever seen
                all you have to do is sign
                   right here on the
                          . . . . dotted line

ACTION

10 5
San Bernardino
Santa Ana
11 NORTH
Pasadena Fwy
Pasadena
11 SOUTH
Harbor Fwy
San Pedro
11 Pasadena Fwy
Pasadena
42

FREEWAY

it's

much faster and more fun

to chase the sun

by freeway

tripping down

sleek hemi-charged lanes of chance and number

pursued by

road demons

wailing primal incantations

in frantic parameters of

faustian rhyme

can you dig it

salesmen lawyers and engineers

housewives hookers and financiers

seeking

crystal visions of form and function

at

the junction of

neon moonscapes and strawberry fields

casting

parabolic shadows onto

neat dichondra lawns

and the spirit of 76

each freeway sign and interchange

refines the flow of

mobil seekers

blessing each

to find his (her) way again

among sunlit corridors

of

ozone and nitrogen

diablo!

the

steel-drivin' men

who

chased the sun

hammered their spikes

till the west was won

their muscle and sweat

is with us yet

in

frontier tales and endless rails

nowadays

travellers who once made the scene from

little rock and abilene

prefer the serenity of transsonic jet

and

the anonymity of the freeway set

they know

the best things in life are free

hyped by a bullish gnp

in its apogee

diesel-rumbling through

the cajon pass

chengaste!

those

steel-drivin' men with their railroad tracks

carried the west on plebian backs

the record shows they

laid the way

for

the union southern and santa fe

PS
CONTINENTAL AIR
AIR WEST
PSA

LAX

fly me
said
the dying queen
to her courtiers
from
the palace scene
and mourning they viewed
her closing eyes
and vowed
to fly
the friendly skies

united
they fashioned
a blazing path high above
the neon-wired wilderness
in
vapor-training twilight sky
surely
the only way to fly

and when
the royal birds touch down
from
tokyo and gotham town
the
computer techs
of LAX
proceed to count from one to ten
and
launch the birds
back up
again

SIGNAL
AHEAD

SURFERS

as
the waves break
toward
the pebbled shore
like
the undulating belly of a seasoned whore
bronze demons ride
their cresting walls
pursued
by piercing
siren calls

echelons
of
this surfing horde
astride
their swift and streamlined board
bear down
with lusting primal moves
along
their briny ocean grooves

and when
they mount their final wave
with
toes curled and sinews taut
a
hovering fireball dips its head
hanging ten
down the pipeline
jamming
through
shimmering rainbow sprays and
endless summers

TRIBAL DANCE

years ago

when

arthur murray was king

and

lawrence welk was happening

mom and dad could have a ball

on

bourbon 'n branch

and geritol

they didn't know

the times

they were a changin'

down on blueberry hill

among

heartbreak hotels and throbbing juke boxes

wailing new rhythms

through

moonlit smoky hollows and carolina pines

for

lightnin'-zapped good old boys

and rump-thumpin' black foxes sock-hopping

around the clock

with each dissenting

dixie morn

it was happenin' baby
it was now not maybe

down south

in the

cotton bowl

in the land of soul

and

ku-kluxees and black-eyed peas
chittlins 'n' grits 'n' bar-b-q pits

                                        great balls of fire
grey-flanneled preppies
by the dozen
joined their cousins in
blue suede shoes rocking the blues
through
guitar-twanging bars
while
superstars
crossed the mersey
slouching toward
gotham's inner-city canyons
where
lonely surfer boys couldn't get no
satisfaction
twisting the night away
the day
the walrus made the scene
with
a cosmic tambourine
for
the girl with kaleidoscope eyes
warping
through
diamond-studded skies
10,000 light years from home
in
fender-driven configurations with
a white rabbit

and the vision
that
was planted

in my brain

still

remains

and remains

and remains

and remains

and

COLISEUM

sundays

when

the winter sun hangs low over

the big orange

a perennial chorus of deep-throated roars

rumbles

its tribal blood-yell within

these coliseum walls

subtle rotarians and undercover social workers

wired to

low-profile corporate intrigue

and gucci bags

hoist the flags of competition

pumping hot and wild once-removed

from

youthful body counts

ah but

my my

down here

on the playing field

explosive formations

yield

a flurry of

red dogs traps and churning thighs

precision bombs and third down tries

sweeping and streaking

down

euphoric sidelines

toward

primal post patterns

FAST BREAK

perpetual motion
is four quarters of
the LA lakers
in heat
having a wham-bam night

the forum's finest
racking up the score
along
the shimmering hardwood floor
execute
precision moves
while
a packed house grooves
their fluid-free surreal
ballet

dead shots
swish
the net
while
gleaming shields of sweat
ride
the players
driving up and under flailing arms
wih closing seconds marking time
as
wired patrons climb
their seats
for

the final buzzer

BODY ENGLISH

if your old lady
doesn't turn you on
or
your libido is ready for
forest lawn

if
you somehow never got the feel
of lovemaking
without
a good housekeeping seal

if
you're hung up in rituals of family
imposed by a prosaic majority
if
you're into being a grabber and a climber
then
you've got a problem
old timer

but you just might turn yourself around
and
begin to hear the siren's sound
come watch
these ladies of erotic form
turn-on
your head with exotic gyrations
until your very own
tumescent vibrations

move you to
go home and
perform

$2 SHOW

HOLLYWOOD PARK

the
hefty fortunes lost and won
blessed
by the california sun
are sweet addictive happenings
for those who play
the sport of kings

snorting roaring thoroughbreds
wired to
fistfuls of dollars
race along
the mirrored track
for
debutante and market maven

the daily double takes its toll
of
housewives in a sporting role
while aging salesmen handicap
with
cigar ashes on their lap

speeding past
the finish line
a longshot
gives
the v-shaped sign
as
losers raise their cutty sark
and toast the ninth
at
hollywood park

JOGGERS

the
cholesterol count is high
old warriors
driven
by market demons
never make it
past fifty
like they used to

sleepy fluids
snake their way heavily
through
origami-like tissues
a dim memory of
wild and vibrant trips
fading
into
tired layers
of
sludge

once again
the center
pumps in time
to
youthful rhythym
as joggers
puff their way
through
wheezing emphysema
toward
an apoplectic vision

The

ten to one
if
you're new in town
you'll want to
get your head together
and
have some fun and chase the sun

voiding the corporate bladder
and
miming the social patter
are only
part of the scene
a nightly rendezvous
with
an amorous ingenue
makes young bodies
lean and mean

so
come join us in the happy hour
grab a drink and circulate
in pursuit
of
an evening's playmate
a chosen glance
can mean romance
then
it's wine and dine
and
head
for home

HEAVYWEIGHTS

jarring jabs and jolting hooks
and the
fury of a murderous swing
screaming fans waving
fisted hands
for the heavyweights in the bloody ring

the tension grows
with the pounding blows and
grunting primal sounds
as patrons roar while keeping score
will it go
the fifteen rounfds

with each new crunch
of a body punch
the ringside viewers bare their soul and
view with ease
the weakening knees
as
the pounding takes its toll

it's sro
at the knockout blow
the winner's fans are on their feet
the loser then gets his
count of ten
and walks
his
lonely street

BIKERS

when

attila the hun meets ghengis khan

and caligula joins the borgia clan and

the desert reeks of gasoline

from

rommel's panzer korps

and the ss is stoned on mescaline from

the corner candy store

when

everywhere for miles around

both bird and beast confront the sound

of

righteous harleys spewing flame

bellowing fire in satan's name

then

house shake and palm trees quake

and mothers lock heir doors

as

the southland folk are eating smoke

from the roaring 74s

and

all the day and through the night

both sun and moon record the sight

of

the last frontiersmen of the west

roaring flat-out while envied by the rest

whose lives are tied

to a medium-cool countryside

sharing vicarious dreams

as they watch

the bikers

R -- I-- D-- E

CENTER COURT

a game of inches

and

split-second moves

strategy and nerves and cross-court grooves

form and grace

with a service ace

put it all together

on

center court

love is

never having to say

ad out

net volleys are what the game is about

a token lob for the gallery mob

then a

really righteous backcourt

smash

through every set

of

motion and sweat

the demon-strokes continue

match point is won

with

the setting sun

winding down

an afternoon

on

center court

SOUTH
NORTH
CALIFORNIA
11
CALIFORNIA
11
SOUTH
Harbor Fwy
NORTH

FRESH
CORN
12
FOR
1.00

TRAVELLERS

do you know the way

along

a funky yellow brick road

strewn

with star-burst visions and cosmic rhyme

pulsing through linear declensions

of

polymorphous tits and acne pits

toward

rainbow-colored mansions

in the land of oz

can you find the way

past

fluted colonnades and marketplace charades

and

crusted ritual spawned by

generational gaps of tired information

howling down shadowy corridors of deja vu

mirror-shifting

in points of you

along

imploding vectors of softening focus

on the late late show

will you show the way

for

a generation of youthful seekers

on the go

while scanned by selectronic eyes

is it

passes

:::through:::

RITUAL

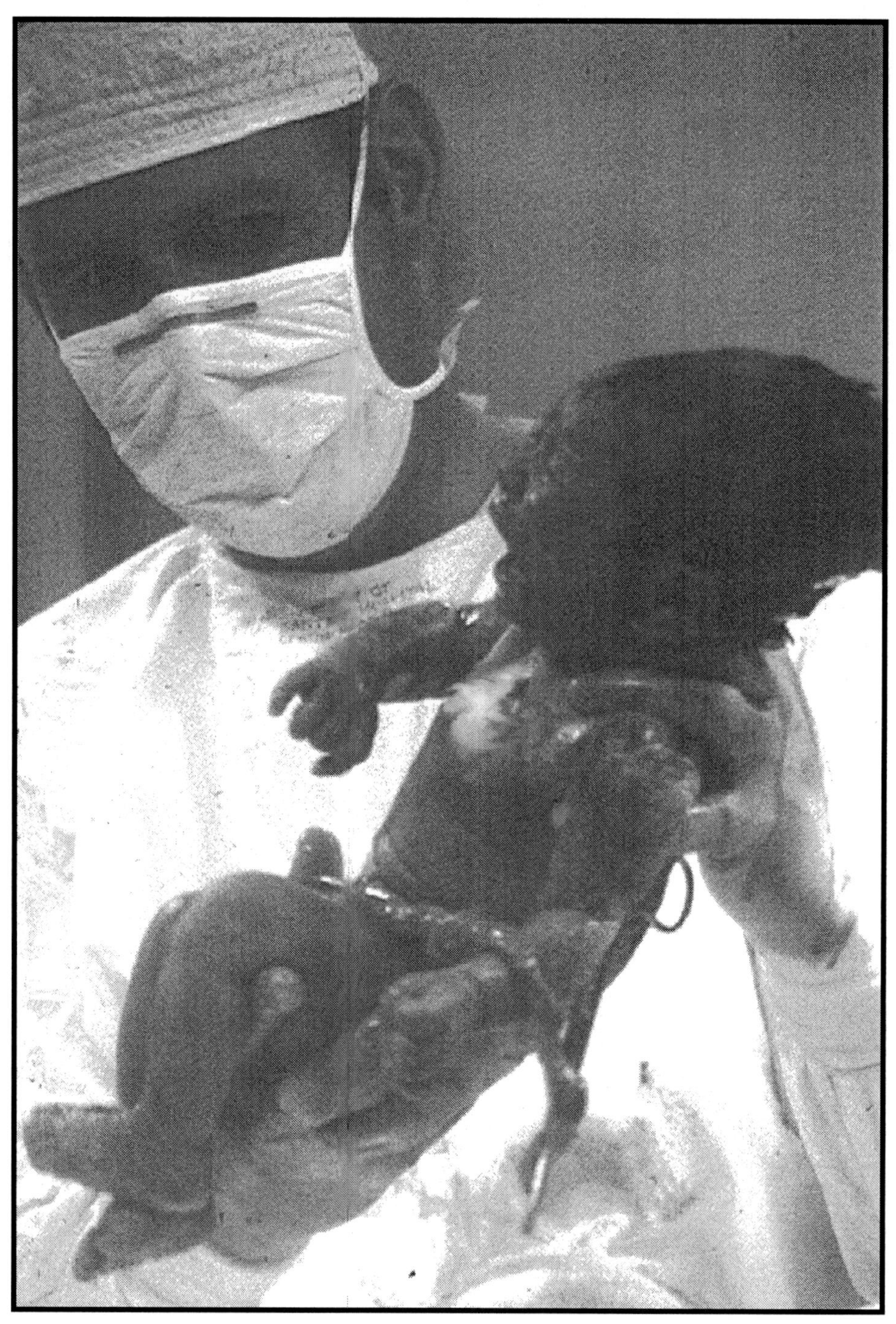

DELIVERY

what
rough beast
newly sprung from his
foetal sac
amid
swaddling fluids
in its
pristine manger
having viewed the primal vision
in repose
now shrieks his
dies irae

what brave new world
awaits his rage
unweaned as yet from
tribal wise men
what
binary computer page
programs
his
earthly playpen

what
dialectic synergy
will evolve upon his
mother's knee
what
bio-circuitry
will groove
his
cosmic legacy

will he be a stranger

will he
fit
the common plan
or
will he be
a

SUPERMAN

4B37A
BRAIN
SALAD
SURGE

THE CONSUMERS

in
their finest hour
children of a new age
jog through rituals of
faustian overkill
tuning in
to
mellowing drummers
synch-wired to the land of oz

they hear
the siren-wail of corporate demons
casting
parabolic shadows
on the marketplace
where the race
for inner space
inherited by
meek subscribers of
cosmic ditties of no tune
did soon
implode in visions of
living color

linear generations
passing down
felonious deeds of no trust
renewing dubious issues
short on maturity
seek
perpetuity
while
tomorrow's children
weaned on tits of scacity
share
an ominous load
along
a funky yellow brick road
consumed by
the torch of deja vu

and as faustian man
is laid to rest
by
electronic globular request
a host of
consumer kings and queens
frolic all the while
in a
mischievous computer's

smile

All Saints' Church
PROTESTANT EPISCOPAL

BEACON LIGHT
BAPTIST CHURCH
The Hiram C. Jones PASTOR
ORDER of SERVICE
SUNDAY SCHOOL   9:45
MORNING WORSHIP   11:15
B.T.U.   6:00
NIGHT SERVICE   7:00
PRAYER TEACHING   7:00

THE WORSHIPPERS

through
the rain forest darkly
the hiss and roar of
savage elements waging war
cowed the soul
of
primeval man
as he sat huddled among
his
tribal clan

long-forgotten incantations
and
midnight howling celebrations
overcame
the primal fear
of angry demons hovering near
but
left intact
the awful fact
that he would someday
die

deriving from
this mortal dread
a vision of
universal godhead
tribal man
then
sought his place
among
the angel dust of
outer space

he
sought to share
celestial time
with a
mud-spattered pantomime
he found instead
a
faustian void
himself
its
spaced-out anthropoid

and
since
that fateful happening
historic man
has
done his thing
with
skyward-reaching monuments
and
divine-inspired governments
mirror-shifting
territorial imperatives
for
the maddening crowd
whose
daily bread
is fed
in
quasar dreams

HOUSEWIVES AND HOOKERS

when the sun first rose
on
tribal man
he and his brothers
devised a plan
to leave the rain forest and
found a race
of civilized beings
to replace
their ape-ancestral clan

so they scraped off the mud
from
their hairy limbs
chanted a few primitive hymns
gathered up their women and tools
and split

now the womenfolk
of
this historic span
dating back from the tribal clan
have kept their ledger of events
each written
in fear and impotence

the entries show
wih great precision
the male-imposed division
of their sex
into those for family and
foxy ladies for harlotry

where
the housewife
has been
the mother of invention
the hooker
has fanned
the spark of intention
serving as catalyst
to
countless promoters
from
the punic wars to general motors

now
it's saturday night
in
beverly hills
and the streets are lined with
mercedes grilles
as
every lounge and hotel bar
is holding
an
investment seminar
        far-out ventures
and
financial schemes
all born
in the heat of
promoters' dreams

and while
the housewife is safe
in her
suburban chateau

watching
the late late show
the hooker
is
making a
different scene
helping keep

america
green

SENIOR CITIZENS

the
old folks here
don't guzzle beer
as
they watch the mets
in action
nor do they spend their time
watching the climb
of the dow jones
for
their satisfaction

no quiet desperation
for
the old folks here
knowing their final hour
is near
unlike their eastern neighbors
rattling mental sabers
of
freud and marx and baseball scores
behind the safety
of
double-locked doos

the old folks here are
hip
to the name of the game
as they watch

their
slow-fading flame
flicker and then come to rest
in
psychedelic sunset
here
out west
they know
the time they spent
as
citizens in retirement
was
free time
grooving
the cosmic freeays
and
opalescent canyons
of
boss city

SUPERSTARS

the music lives
said
the infant queen
as
she jumped from
her crib
on
the palace green
and
the patter of her tiny
feet
in step
with
a mellow
tribal beat
passed
through
the crystal door
to
its fiery
rhythmic core

and
the vapor that her blood
became
was a vision
of

her former name
as
patterns sifting
through
her self
on a
shifting
charismatic
shelf
turned on
even more
the rockers
rocking
at her
side
and then
the infant queen
died

although
it is said

SUPERSTARS
LIVE
FOREVER

COUNTY BARS

few can know
the pain
borne by
the children of cain
whose
existential sin
as
disenfranchised kin
was set by
almighty whim

their legacy
sustains from birth
the mark
of
undervalued worth
a divine slight
that
certified
their primal father's
fratricide

their
instant rage
subsides somewhat
with
age
and perennial visits
past

neat dichondra lawns
and
neocorporate yawns
and
superstars
inside

again
these county bars

TRIPPING

old
encrusted
rigid forms
have
a strange cocoonlike way
by
shutting out
the
light of day
of
giving birth
where
birth is due
without necessarily
meaning to

or
is it some
bionic quirk
where
primeval demons
lurk
howling
along
midnight convoluted tracks
before reason
without time
in

silent siren tones
of
stroboscopic
angel dust

the seeker
seeks
within himself
the
long-forgotten shelf
of
many faces
and
warping through
grooves
a faint residue
of
nameless places
before reason
without time
toward
a crystal vision
of
the
universal pantomime

SWINGERS

old macdonald
had a farm
and
on his farm
he had
some
deep-throated fillies
who
pranced and danced
and
did a whole number of
fancy steps
with
hard-breathing stud stallions
in
multi-layered signs of the zodiac
while
all the other
barnyard animals
picked up their cues
put on
their high-stepping shoes
and
commenced to rock and roll
around
old macdonald's
far-out
maypole

you too can
cruise

your neighborhood bar
get wild and wet
in
your jaguar
you
could be
your very own
swinging superstar
or
would you rather be

      an aardvark

LEX
JUSTICE
ES COUNTY C

COURTROOM

toward
a new millenium
gladiators
rush the arena to
ride
a carousel
of
forbidden dreams
and
ponzi schemes
valued
by
their scarcity

the new age
wears
its basic flaw
from the old world tree of
common law
whose
political philosophy
sags
beneath the weight of
crusted ritual
following
cumulative linear declensions
within
cabalistic chauvinistic dimensions
toward
electronic gateways
of psychic afterbirth

before too long
some
far-out tribunal
sitting
in
surreal binary chambers
is
going to pass on
the
long-awaited
unspoken
word

so far
the jury is
still

out

DUTY

old soldiers
never die

generations
of
good old boys
barefoot ruddy-cheeked native sons
flush with
pioneer visions of glorious empire
and
southern comfort
seek their final
resting place
here
under the california sun

they were there
pumping
hot and wild
in
smoky ravines and cratered slopes and coral shores
shouting
primal blood yells
with
fixed bayonets and transsonic jets
conducting
celestial missions impossible
to
seek and destroy
enemies
of
common law and contributory affluence and the rights of
free rotarians

CINEMA

BRIGHT ANGELS

consider
the lilies of the field
neither
do they spin
nor chase their opposite kin
down
patterned corridors of
celluloid lust

grooving
twilight paths
in
lavender and lace
the aging grace of yesterday's queens
shudders through
a
macluhanesque gap
clutching its throat watching judy and ethel on
the late late show

while
a new breed
epicene plowboys and virginia slim glitterbelles
prance
in tribal pirouettes
rocking the light fantastic
from
fire island to the bel-air gate
streaking
brite-bunned and bushy-tailed
through
quadrasonic sunsets
toward the ever-sunny
land of oz

DEPARTMENT OF
RESOURCES DEVEL

JOB INFORMATION
CENTER
2
C1

UNEMPLOYMENT LINE

far-out ponzi schemes
have a way of always keeping
one step ahead of
demons of the marketplace

overnight
mythical gremlins
have built a stairway to heaven
with bulging unemployment lines
some say
it's a fool's paradise
but
that weekly check is awful nice
when
little willie needs new braces
or
the judge is making faces
at your
unpaid traffic fines

so come stand in line and see - -

forgotten movie queens and strung-out ex-marines
real estate tycoons and nite-club buffoons
restauranteurs and entrepreneurs aerospace designers and regretful co-signors
social engineers and construction overseers mortgage men and garbage men
a disc jockey cook and a narc who's eyeing you
an uncle cousin and an ex-wife or two

they had a position open last week
as janitor
the position's still unfilled you see
cause all the applicants had
a phd

100
LEAN BEDS
HOT & COLD
SHOWERS
WEEKLY RATES
NEXT
DOOR
304½
DI
WA
JE

CLOSED
HOURS
EMERGENCY CALL

5TH STREET

you might think it strange
that the old boys on
5th street
in shabby clothes
have anything in common with those at the LA country club
(while you won't find them listed in who's who
they're members of the leisure class too)

they share with their more affluent kin
the luxury of original sin
possessing a totally solipsistic view
knowing at an early age the futility of a daily wage and from
the many called are chosen few

to the old boys on 5th street
when they were young
the future spoke with a foreign tongue
they heard instead a musical beat
an ancient rhythym of primitive feet
and crude instruments lost in time
when the tribal race was in its prime
a forgotten language of
crackling campfires and howls in the night and midnight rituals

the old boys on 5th street
didn't go to the moon they went much further
down countless roads searching for
a stone a leaf an unfound door and finding
nothing

nor marker nor hopeful sign
but the naked truth
in a bottle of
wine

TOGETHER

you can enjoy me

as i am

and

i can see you

as you are

and

we can both see and enjoy

what

we each enjoy

in

one another

time recalled is time unravelled

when

you and i could see

the far side of eternity

and

night was day

and day blazed like the bright core

of

a billion suns and more

and

we never heard the demons roar

now

we lie on grassy slopes

sharing dubious hopes

with

our tribal brethren

all together

mellowed by sweet dreams and

the california weather

MOURNING

trouble is
you get close to people
sharing
psychic gifts of
love and trust
to gain
a
random pass
through
a rainbow-colored glass

trouble is
they
come at you all at once
blood and kinfolk friends and neighbors
honey-mouth and angel tits and
snarling philosophic old men
brawling balling wheezing puking
cooing multiple-climaxing mind-zapping

god's own
barefoot children

rolling
celestial numbers
for
good old boys
on
the back line

beware
the pit boss

GENERATION

the center seeks
to
know itself

configurations
probing
random angel dust
pulse through patterns of
chance and number
toward a crystal junction
of
form and function

the torch of
deja vu
beams
its binary message code through
biogenetic circuits
transmitting primal imprints
higher up
darwinian modes
of
sons and daughters
chasing
solar wavelengths
down
frontier freeways
in search of
a rolling stone a leaf of grass a psychedelic door
to turn
the universal
existential
trick

BROWN
FOR GOVERNOR

GETTING OFF

he

thrusting full and firm

kinetic visions of glorious empire

tempered by

common law and contributory affluence

ascending

sleek generational corridors of sound and fury

transmitting divine revelations

in deja vu

and she

receiving firm and fully

primal penetrations

in

faustian code sweetened by

feminine mystique and egalitarian chic

enfolding

prime monolithic peaks

in confirmation

beaming

crystal tones of euphoria

together mellowing

with

satin strokes

pulsing toward

shimmering dimensions

streaking

through

the looking glass

in

galactic fantastic showers

of

:::angel dust:::

CIRCUITRY

deals are made
in the shade
of
ornately chiselled columns
and
frescoed porticos
within
teakwood anterooms
and
binary computer wombs
where
a rose
is not always
a
rose

linear generations
wired to
forms of antiquity
ride
cresting walls of
scarcity
along
yellow brick roads
of
tax-sheltered modes
toward
the eternal gnp

in
its infinite
apogee

:::now:::
within
the eye of
instant time
corporate norms
and
tribal forms
converge
in
synergistic
deja vu
exchanging binary gifts
in
mellow shifts
through
milli-micro paths
of circuitry
in search of
the grand differential of fusion
to turn
the universal
existential
trick

VISION

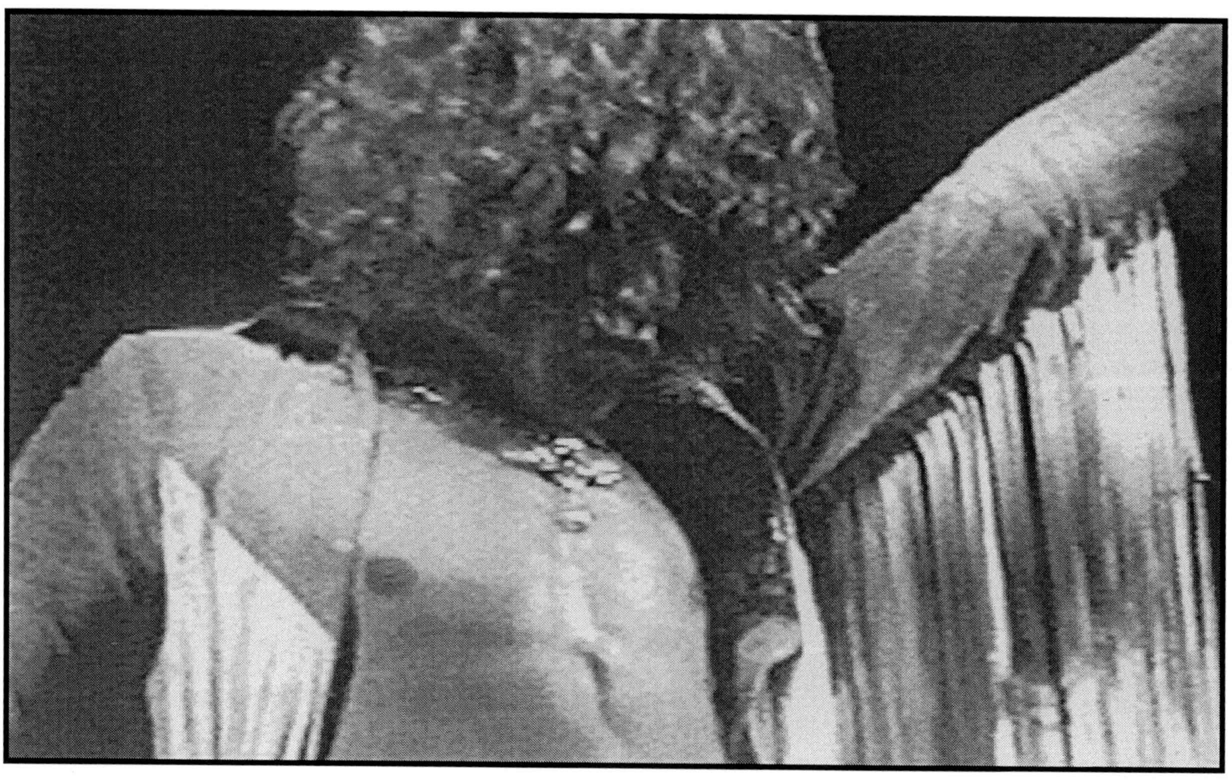

THE GATHERING OF
THE TRIBES

somehow
the word got out
somehow
a moving finger
touched
a random primal switch
as
the restless of the earth
tuned in
their global circuits
and heard
there was to be

A SECOND COMING

and some came
running

sun-bronzed travellers
with
gentle grinning faces
weather-scarred and weary
from long
on the road

angelic runaways
from
mom and dad and junior hi
with sun-shaded lashes

in
patchwork fashions from
the house of straus

campus faculty lions
roaring fiery rhetoric of
neo-marx-marcuse-macluhan-and-mailer
for
academic sheep in wolves' clothing
gagging on their freudian knot
and howling at the womb

children of the sun
corn-fed brite-eyed and bushy-tailed
mastercharge card-carrying
revolutionaries in exile from
neat dichondra lawns

intrepid travellers
day-glo yippies and junior heads
outstaring the sun
tossing poppy seeds
to feed the pigs

captain america
hyping
tangerine-flake-baby mellow bikers
with
super electric kool aid
breathing candy-acid hellfire
down
lysergical cannabistic sunflower-powered
freeway-ay-ay-ay-ay-ay-ay-ay-
! zzzzzzzzzzzzzzzzzzzzzz !

and some came

riding

hypermod entrepreneurs
with heavy bread
grooving
double-knit stereo vibes
come to mount
the counterculture
and
bring home the big beat
on a platter

media wizards
with
feedback gear
synch-wired to the land of oz
to tell it like it was
in
instant deja vu
for ethical
puritans foundation-grant sociologists
and
armchair con III types

the man
bearing presence
in many forms
friendly fuzz in choppers
riding shotgun
in the sky
FB eyes and long-haired narcs
finding
double-coverage blowing in the wind
with
CIA lads in drag

and some came

limping

right-on panthers
and brown berets
purple-badged and shotgun-scarred
by
irate rotarians hoarding
primal trust deeds

bleeding sisters
chained
to
seven pillars of blue-chip-stamped
suburban serfdom
and
corporate-chauvinist steno pools

doe-eyed gays
and
plump daughters of bilitis
newly sprung
from claustrophobic closets
chanting

bi-bi ms amerikan pie

purple-stumped amputees
and
wheelchair vets
ambushed by charly
between halftime commercials
in living color

tribal warriors and maidens
of great red chiefs
whooping
down cybernetic inner-city canyons
on the rtd

and some came

crawling

the lost
and disenfranchised
and broken in spirit
retching through
ash heaps of limp desperation
on
ancient hands and knees

midnight limbo-dwellers
neither consumer fish nor corporate fowl
skidding down
neon moonscapes
incognito

and
boys and girls of all seasons
nailed
upside down in time and space
cast
into outer darkness unweeping
whose
only sin was
being true
to their
primal vision

slowly
the sun warmed
the gathering
in its rise
toward high noon

cosmic vibrations

crackled
among the tribes
touching
bare flesh
and
naked electric nerve tips
in
flower birth celebration

apocalyptic chords
and
gut-free lyric
amplified
to
celestial decibels
consumed
the seven seals of euphoria
and turned on
the rock spirits

heads
were flowing
in amoebic shapes
10,000,000 light years high
billowing
in and out of
time
to
dancing young bodies

as
the sun began
its
downward arc

179

the chorus swirled
higher and higher
exorcising howling demons
with
dionysian incantations
marking
surreal time
for

::: THE COMING:::

fiery waves of energy
stroked

the gathering
to
electromagnetic superpitch
while
micro-wired media wizards
from the land of oz

tuned
selectronic scanners to
record the event and
waited

as

the sun dropped
below
a far horizon

the gathering grew silent
no sound nothing
as they waited through
the cold night
within
the tribal fields
and
along the road and
nobody ever
showed

VISION IN MOTION

vision
began to feed upon
itself
with
hardware from
the corporate shelf
and wore
an instant skin
of
circuitry
integrating
a great society
exploding
outward
from its seams
along
psychomagnetic beams
curving
inward
through the core
of
an asiatic war
blowing
psychedelic heads
from
academic flower beds
as
ghetto children
rocked the street
to a
rhythmic tribal beat
outside

the cybernetic race
for
a step
in outer space
giant
in the
corporate mind
committed to find
the key
to
perpetuity
for a
stoned majority
silently
feeding
binary scrolls
with
fragmented
life-roles
for
the master read-out

ANGEL DUST

first

the players became

viewers

and lost their touch

and then

the viewers became players

and

it didn't matter much

which

frame of reference was

your preference

from

a shifting point of you

descending

men and women

shattering

specious origins

viewing eternity

with

backward-winding clocks

from

fragmented absolutes and pulsing convolutes

found

the vd rate

among

thirteen-year-olds

alarming

ancient mariners

walking

a constant planck

found
apollo's corridor to
a spaced-out bank
dealing
lunar parcels far
from pershing square
where
a pigeon-feeding plumber finds
avogadro's number
is paying
ten-to-one

a flock of golden jacks and jills
eats
rainbow-colored daffodils
from
suborbital rose bowl floats
while
saturn-boosting physicists
od
on freeze-dried catalysts
between
each hip trajectory
of
the dow jones

scanned
by neat electrons
the children of bangladesh
find
calcutta garbage scraps
finger-licking good
while
mideastern farmers

in
hash brown brotherhood
urge
poppy-powered price support

third world natives
and deserted nomads
can't find
the key
to
their playboy pads
amid the scarcity outside
the gold mirage
hyped
by european
arbitrage
daily

gaily gaily
the
great binary god computer
gathered
bits and fragments
fed
by programming parents
wired
to global circuits
integrating
processed forms
within
neocorporate norms
like
an electronic massive
roto-rooter

somehow
the readings didn't
jive and
the control panel
took a dive

as
all systems read

OVERLOAD!

the circuits then were
localized
and
found to be
polarized
and
would not yield
their frozen field
except
for some cryptic message code

:::ANGEL DUST:::

COSMIC BIRTH

through
the looking glass
slowly

the dance began

warping
along
shadowy corridors
of
mom and dad and junior hi
and
good old boys
riding shotgun in the sky
tripping
past
neon moonscapes
and
strawberry fields
forever
to sever
unbiblical chords
with
primal boards
hi-riding
the cosmic surf
thrusting
full and firm
through
charismatic satin channels
of
mellow thighs and kaleidoscope eyes

balling

the milky way

in

quadrasonic last tangos

mellowing

toward

shimmering new dimensions

imploding time-warping mirror-shifting

shadow and substance

multiple-climaxing

in

a semen spray

of

hyperbolic angel dust

with

brothers and sisters

chasing

a rolling stone a leaf of grass a

psychedelic door

down

frontier freeways

of

cosmic interchange

toward

a

crystal junction

of

form and function

mirror-shifting

the very

::core:::

of

generation

where

tomorrow's message code
the
eucharistic vision
of
meek subscribers
booming
cosmic ditties of no tune
did soon
implode
the universal field
beaming
galactic fantastic

perpetuity

through
the looking glass

it
isn't very
hard to find
if
you don't mind
travelling
for
as long as it takes

baby

MARK ST. GEORGE lives in Los Angeles. He has a background in Real Estate, Law and Financial Markets.